MATH NOTEBOOK
& JOURNAL
FOR ADULT STUDENTS

BY COACHING FOR BETTER LEARNING

"The powerful thinkers are those who make connections, think logically, and use space, data, and numbers creatively." – Jo Boaler

This Math Notebook & Journal is designed to help adult students take good notes, define math concepts, reflect on math ideas, and plan their practice time.

Name: ____

Lesson: _______________________________ **Date:** __________ **Time:** _________

Objectives: ____

Notes or Important Information

Math Concepts

Lesson Summary (Math ideas, principles, or formulas)

Learning Reflection

Math procedures and methods that I learned.	Math concepts and formula I learned.

Questions that I have.

1.
2.
3.
4.
5.

What I need to reread or review.

What I need help with.

Action Steps

What I will prepare for next class (Math Assignment)

Math questions for next class.

My target practice time.

Reward for meeting my practice

example: one hour of TV show

What I will do better in the next class.

General Notes

Lesson: _________________________________ **Date:** ___________ **Time:** _________

Objectives: ____

Notes or Important Information

Math Concepts

Lesson Summary (Math ideas, principles, or formulas)

Learning Reflection

Math procedures and methods that I learned.	Math concepts and formula I learned.

Questions that I have.

1.
2.
3.
4.
5.

What I need to reread or review.

What I need help with.

Action Steps

What I will prepare for next class (Math Assignment)

Math questions for next class.

My target practice time.

Reward for meeting my practice
example: one hour of TV show

What I will do better in the next class.

General Notes

Lesson: _________________________________ **Date:** __________ **Time:** _________

Objectives: ____

Notes or Important Information

Math Concepts

Lesson Summary (Math ideas, principles, or formulas)

Learning Reflection

<table>
<tr>
<td>Math procedures and methods that I learned.</td>
<td>Math concepts and formula I learned.</td>
</tr>
</table>

Questions that I have.

1.
2.
3.
4.
5.

What I need to reread or review.

What I need help with.

Action Steps

What I will prepare for next class (Math Assignment)

Math questions for next class.

My target practice time.

Reward for meeting my practice
example: one hour of TV show

What I will do better in the next class.

General Notes

Lesson: _______________________________ **Date:** __________ **Time:** __________

Objectives: ____

Notes or Important Information

Math Concepts

Lesson Summary (Math ideas, principles, or formulas)

Learning Reflection

Math procedures and methods that I learned.	Math concepts and formula I learned.

Questions that I have.

1.
2.
3.
4.
5.

What I need to reread or review.

What I need help with.

Action Steps

What I will prepare for next class (Math Assignment)

Math questions for next class.

My target practice time.

Reward for meeting my practice
example: one hour of TV show

What I will do better in the next class.

General Notes

Lesson: _______________________________ **Date:** _________ **Time:** _________

Objectives: _______________________________

Notes or Important Information

Math Concepts

Lesson Summary (Math ideas, principles, or formulas)

Learning Reflection

Math procedures and methods that I learned.

Math concepts and formula I learned.

Questions that I have.

1.
2.
3.
4.
5.

What I need to reread or review.

What I need help with.

Action Steps

What I will prepare for next class (Math Assignment)

Math questions for next class.

My target practice time.

Reward for meeting my practice
example: one hour of TV show

What I will do better in the next class.

General Notes

Lesson: _______________________________ **Date:** __________ **Time:** __________

Objectives: ____

Notes or Important Information

Math Concepts

Lesson Summary (Math ideas, principles, or formulas)

Learning Reflection

<table>
<tr><td>Math procedures and methods that I learned.</td><td>Math concepts and formula I learned.</td></tr>
</table>

Questions that I have.

1.
2.
3.
4.
5.

What I need to reread or review.

What I need help with.

Action Steps

What I will prepare for next class (Math Assignment)

Math questions for next class.

My target practice time.

Reward for meeting my practice
example: one hour of TV show

What I will do better in the next class.

General Notes

Lesson: ______________________________ **Date:** _________ **Time:** _________

Objectives: ______________________________

Notes or Important Information

Math Concepts

Lesson Summary (Math ideas, principles, or formulas)

Learning Reflection

<table>
<tr><td>Math procedures and methods that I learned.</td><td>Math concepts and formula I learned.</td></tr>
</table>

Questions that I have.

1.
2.
3.
4.
5.

What I need to reread or review.

What I need help with.

Action Steps

What I will prepare for next class (Math Assignment)

Math questions for next class.

My target practice time.

Reward for meeting my practice
example: one hour of TV show

What I will do better in the next class.

General Notes

Lesson: _______________________________ **Date:** _________ **Time:** _________

Objectives: ____

Notes or Important Information

Math Concepts

Lesson Summary (Math ideas, principles, or formulas)

Learning Reflection

<table>
<tr><td>Math procedures and methods that I learned.</td><td>Math concepts and formula I learned.</td></tr>
<tr><td></td><td></td></tr>
</table>

Questions that I have.

1.
2.
3.
4.
5.

What I need to reread or review.

What I need help with.

Action Steps

What I will prepare for next class (Math Assignment)

Math questions for next class.

My target practice time.

Reward for meeting my practice
example: one hour of TV show

What I will do better in the next class.

General Notes

Lesson: _______________________________ **Date:** __________ **Time:** __________

Objectives: ____

Notes or Important Information

____
____
____
____
____
____
____
____
____
____
____
____

Math Concepts

Lesson Summary (Math ideas, principles, or formulas)

____
____
____
____
____

Learning Reflection

<table>
<tr><td>

Math procedures and methods that I learned.

</td><td>

Math concepts and formula I learned.

</td></tr>
</table>

Questions that I have.

1.
2.
3.
4.
5.

What I need to reread or review.

What I need help with.

Action Steps

What I will prepare for next class (Math Assignment)

Math questions for next class.

My target practice time.

Reward for meeting my practice
example: one hour of TV show

What I will do better in the next class.

General Notes

Lesson: _______________________________ **Date:** __________ **Time:** _________

Objectives: ____

Notes or Important Information

Math Concepts

Lesson Summary (Math ideas, principles, or formulas)

Learning Reflection

<table>
<tr><td>Math procedures and methods that I learned.</td><td>Math concepts and formula I learned.</td></tr>
</table>

Questions that I have.

1.
2.
3.
4.
5.

What I need to reread or review.

What I need help with.

Action Steps

What I will prepare for next class (Math Assignment)

Math questions for next class.

My target practice time.

Reward for meeting my practice
example: one hour of TV show

What I will do better in the next class.

General Notes

Lesson: _________________________________ **Date:** __________ **Time:** __________

Objectives: ____

Notes or Important Information

Math Concepts

Lesson Summary (Math ideas, principles, or formulas)

Learning Reflection

<table>
<tr><td>Math procedures and methods that I learned.</td><td>Math concepts and formula I learned.</td></tr>
</table>

Questions that I have.

1.
2.
3.
4.
5.

What I need to reread or review.

What I need help with.

Action Steps

What I will prepare for next class (Math Assignment)

Math questions for next class.

My target practice time.

Reward for meeting my practice
example: one hour of TV show

What I will do better in the next class.

General Notes

Lesson: ___________________________ **Date:** __________ **Time:** __________

Objectives: ____

Notes or Important Information

Math Concepts

Lesson Summary (Math ideas, principles, or formulas)

Learning Reflection

Math procedures and methods that I learned.	Math concepts and formula I learned.

Questions that I have.

1.
2.
3.
4.
5.

What I need to reread or review.

What I need help with.

Action Steps

What I will prepare for next class (Math Assignment)

Math questions for next class.

My target practice time.

Reward for meeting my practice
example: one hour of TV show

What I will do better in the next class.

General Notes

Lesson: _________________________________ **Date:** __________ **Time:** __________

Objectives: ____

Notes or Important Information

Math Concepts

Lesson Summary (Math ideas, principles, or formulas)

Learning Reflection

<table>
<tr>
<td>Math procedures and methods that I learned.</td>
<td>Math concepts and formula I learned.</td>
</tr>
</table>

Questions that I have.

1. ____
2. ____
3. ____
4. ____
5. ____

What I need to reread or review.

What I need help with.

Action Steps

What I will prepare for next class (Math Assignment)

Math questions for next class.

My target practice time.	Reward for meeting my practice
	example: one hour of TV show

What I will do better in the next class.

General Notes

Lesson: _________________________________ **Date:** _________ **Time:** _________

Objectives: ____

Notes or Important Information

Math Concepts

Lesson Summary (Math ideas, principles, or formulas)

Learning Reflection

<table>
<tr><td>Math procedures and methods that I learned.</td><td>Math concepts and formula I learned.</td></tr>
<tr><td></td><td></td></tr>
</table>

Questions that I have.

1.
2.
3.
4.
5.

What I need to reread or review.

What I need help with.

Action Steps

What I will prepare for next class (Math Assignment)

Math questions for next class.

My target practice time.

Reward for meeting my practice
example: one hour of TV show

What I will do better in the next class.

General Notes

Lesson: _________________________________ **Date:** __________ **Time:** _________

Objectives: ____

Notes or Important Information

Math Concepts

Lesson Summary (Math ideas, principles, or formulas)

Learning Reflection

<table>
<tr>
<td>Math procedures and methods that I learned.</td>
<td>Math concepts and formula I learned.</td>
</tr>
</table>

Questions that I have.

1.
2.
3.
4.
5.

What I need to reread or review.

What I need help with.

Action Steps

What I will prepare for next class (Math Assignment)

Math questions for next class.

My target practice time.

Reward for meeting my practice
example: one hour of TV show

What I will do better in the next class.

General Notes

Lesson: _____________________________ **Date:** _________ **Time:** _______

Objectives: _____________________________

Notes or Important Information

Math Concepts

Lesson Summary (Math ideas, principles, or formulas)

Learning Reflection

Math procedures and methods that I learned.	Math concepts and formula I learned.

Questions that I have.

1.
2.
3.
4.
5.

What I need to reread or review.

What I need help with.

Action Steps

What I will prepare for next class (Math Assignment)

Math questions for next class.

My target practice time.

Reward for meeting my practice
example: one hour of TV show

What I will do better in the next class.

General Notes

Lesson: _______________________________ **Date:** __________ **Time:** __________

Objectives: ____

Notes or Important Information

Math Concepts

Lesson Summary (Math ideas, principles, or formulas)

Learning Reflection

<table>
<tr>
<td>Math procedures and methods that I learned.</td>
<td>Math concepts and formula I learned.</td>
</tr>
</table>

Questions that I have.

1.
2.
3.
4.
5.

What I need to reread or review.

What I need help with.

Action Steps

What I will prepare for next class (Math Assignment)

Math questions for next class.

My target practice time.

Reward for meeting my practice
example: one hour of TV show

What I will do better in the next class.

General Notes

Lesson: _______________________________ **Date:** ___________ **Time:** _________

Objectives: ____

Notes or Important Information

Math Concepts

Lesson Summary (Math ideas, principles, or formulas)

Learning Reflection

Math procedures and methods that I learned.	**Math concepts and formula I learned.**

Questions that I have.

1. ____
2. ____
3. ____
4. ____
5. ____

What I need to reread or review.

What I need help with.

Action Steps

What I will prepare for next class (Math Assignment)

Math questions for next class.

My target practice time.

Reward for meeting my practice
example: one hour of TV show

What I will do better in the next class.

General Notes

Lesson: _______________________________ **Date:** __________ **Time:** _________
Objectives: ____

Notes or Important Information

Math Concepts

Lesson Summary (Math ideas, principles, or formulas)

Learning Reflection

Math procedures and methods that I learned.	Math concepts and formula I learned.

Questions that I have.

1. ____
2. ____
3. ____
4. ____
5. ____

What I need to reread or review.

What I need help with.

Action Steps

What I will prepare for next class (Math Assignment)

Math questions for next class.

My target practice time.

Reward for meeting my practice

example: one hour of TV show

What I will do better in the next class.

General Notes

Lesson: ___________________________ **Date:** _________ **Time:** _________

Objectives: ___________________________

Notes or Important Information

Math Concepts

Lesson Summary (Math ideas, principles, or formulas)

Learning Reflection

<table>
<tr><td>

Math procedures and methods that I learned.

</td><td>

Math concepts and formula I learned.

</td></tr>
</table>

Questions that I have.

1.
2.
3.
4.
5.

What I need to reread or review.

What I need help with.

Action Steps

What I will prepare for next class (Math Assignment)

Math questions for next class.

My target practice time.

Reward for meeting my practice

example: one hour of TV show

What I will do better in the next class.

General Notes

Lesson: _________________________________ **Date:** ___________ **Time:** _________

Objectives: ____

Notes or Important Information

Math Concepts

Lesson Summary (Math ideas, principles, or formulas)

Learning Reflection

<table>
<tr><td>Math procedures and methods that I learned.</td><td>Math concepts and formula I learned.</td></tr>
</table>

Questions that I have.

1.
2.
3.
4.
5.

What I need to reread or review.

What I need help with.

Action Steps

What I will prepare for next class (Math Assignment)

Math questions for next class.

My target practice time.

Reward for meeting my practice
example: one hour of TV show

What I will do better in the next class.

General Notes

Lesson: _________________________________ **Date:** _________ **Time:** _________

Objectives: ____

Notes or Important Information

Math Concepts

Lesson Summary (Math ideas, principles, or formulas)

Learning Reflection

<table>
<tr><td>Math procedures and methods that I learned.</td><td>Math concepts and formula I learned.</td></tr>
</table>

Questions that I have.

1.
2.
3.
4.
5.

What I need to reread or review.

What I need help with.

Action Steps

What I will prepare for next class (Math Assignment)

Math questions for next class.

My target practice time.

Reward for meeting my practice
example: one hour of TV show

What I will do better in the next class.

General Notes

Lesson: _________________________ **Date:** _________ **Time:** _______

Objectives: ____

Notes or Important Information

Math Concepts

Lesson Summary (Math ideas, principles, or formulas)

Learning Reflection

Math procedures and methods that I learned.	Math concepts and formula I learned.

Questions that I have.

1. ____
2. ____
3. ____
4. ____
5. ____

What I need to reread or review.

What I need help with.

Action Steps

What I will prepare for next class (Math Assignment)

Math questions for next class.

| My target practice time. | Reward for meeting my practice
example: one hour of TV show |

What I will do better in the next class.

General Notes

2022

July

S	M	T	W	T	F	S
					1	2
3	4	5	6	7	8	9
10	11	12	13	14	15	16
17	18	19	20	21	22	23
24	25	26	27	28	29	30
31						

August

S	M	T	W	T	F	S
	1	2	3	4	5	6
7	8	9	10	11	12	13
14	15	16	17	18	19	20
21	22	23	24	25	26	27
28	29	30	31			

September

S	M	T	W	T	F	S
				1	2	3
4	5	6	7	8	9	10
11	12	13	14	15	16	17
18	19	20	21	22	23	24
25	26	27	28	29	30	

October

S	M	T	W	T	F	S
						1
2	3	4	5	6	7	8
9	10	11	12	13	14	15
16	17	18	19	20	21	22
23	24	25	26	27	28	29
30	31					

November

S	M	T	W	T	F	S
		1	2	3	4	5
6	7	8	9	10	11	12
13	14	15	16	17	18	19
20	21	22	23	24	25	26
27	28	29	30			

December

S	M	T	W	T	F	S
				1	2	3
4	5	6	7	8	9	10
11	12	13	14	15	16	17
18	19	20	21	22	23	24
25	26	27	28	29	30	31

Notes

2023

January

S	M	T	W	T	F	S
1	2	3	4	5	6	7
8	9	10	11	12	13	14
15	16	17	18	19	20	21
22	23	24	25	26	27	28
29	30	31				

February

S	M	T	W	T	F	S
			1	2	3	4
5	6	7	8	9	10	11
12	13	14	15	16	17	18
19	20	21	22	23	24	25
26	27	28				

March

S	M	T	W	T	F	S
			1	2	3	4
5	6	7	8	9	10	11
12	13	14	15	16	17	18
19	20	21	22	23	24	25
26	27	28	29	30	31	

April

S	M	T	W	T	F	S
						1
2	3	4	5	6	7	8
9	10	11	12	13	14	15
16	17	18	19	20	21	22
23	24	25	26	27	28	29
30						

May

S	M	T	W	T	F	S
	1	2	3	4	5	6
7	8	9	10	11	12	13
14	15	16	17	18	19	20
21	22	23	24	25	26	27
28	29	30	31			

June

S	M	T	W	T	F	S
				1	2	3
4	5	6	7	8	9	10
11	12	13	14	15	16	17
18	19	20	21	22	23	24
25	26	27	28	29	30	

July

S	M	T	W	T	F	S
						1
2	3	4	5	6	7	8
9	10	11	12	13	14	15
16	17	18	19	20	21	22
23	24	25	26	27	28	29
30	31					

August

S	M	T	W	T	F	S
		1	2	3	4	5
6	7	8	9	10	11	12
13	14	15	16	17	18	19
20	21	22	23	24	25	26
27	28	29	30	31		

September

S	M	T	W	T	F	S
					1	2
3	4	5	6	7	8	9
10	11	12	13	14	15	16
17	18	19	20	21	22	23
24	25	26	27	28	29	30

October

S	M	T	W	T	F	S
1	2	3	4	5	6	7
8	9	10	11	12	13	14
15	16	17	18	19	20	21
22	23	24	25	26	27	28
29	30	31				

November

S	M	T	W	T	F	S
			1	2	3	4
5	6	7	8	9	10	11
12	13	14	15	16	17	18
19	20	21	22	23	24	25
26	27	28	29	30		

December

S	M	T	W	T	F	S
					1	2
3	4	5	6	7	8	9
10	11	12	13	14	15	16
17	18	19	20	21	22	23
24	25	26	27	28	29	30
31						

READING LOG

NO.	BOOK TITLE	START - END DATE	NO. OF PAGES
1			
2			
3			
4			
5			
6			
7			
8			
9			
10			
11			
12			
13			
14			
15			
16			
17			
18			
19			
20			

READING LOG

NO.	BOOK TITLE	START - END DATE	NO. OF PAGES
21			
22			
23			
24			
25			
26			
27			
28			
29			
30			
31			
32			
33			
34			
35			
36			
37			
38			
39			
40			

About Coaching For Better Learning

We promote systematic solutions, innovative ideas, and future-oriented strategies in adult education, workforce development, and vocational training.

We help build systems to lead adult students closer to their dreams.

Send questions or suggestions to teamcbl@coachingforbetterlearning.com.

By the same publisher:

Student textbooks that save instructors time and promote reflective learning to keep learners engaged.

adulteducationhub.com

Website: https://adulteducationhub.com/